SOLITUDES CROWDED WITH LONELINESS

ALSO BY BOB KAUFMAN

The Ancient Rain, Poems 1956–1976

BOB KAUFMAN

SOLITUDES CROWDED WITH LONELINESS

A NEW DIRECTIONS PAPERBOOK

Library of Congress catalog card number: 65–15673
(ISBN: 0-8112-0076-0)

Acknowledgments
Some of these poems, and the "Abomunist" sequence,
first appeared in the San Francisco magazine *Beatitude.*
"Second April" and "Abomunist Manifesto"
were also published as broadsides by Lawrence Ferlinghetti
at City Lights Books, San Francisco. "Bagel Shop Jazz" appeared
in the fourth volume of *The Guinness Book of Poetry,* published
by Putnam & Company Ltd.

Manufactured in the United States of America
New Directions books are printed on acid-free paper
Published in Canada by Penguin Books Canada Limited

EIGHTH PRINTING

SOLITUDES CROWDED WITH LONELINESS

TELEGRAPHIC PREFACE TO KAUFMAN IN SOLITUDES CROWDED WITH LONELINESS OF A BLASTED LONG-DISTANCE RUNNER IM-PROVISING TE DEUMS OF TOTAL RECALL ALONE IN A LEMMING WORLD AMONG ACID VISIONS OF DOORS OPENING INTO MISPLACED BLUE PARADISES OF THE SENSES HIS TONGUE HUNG OUT TO DRY IN IMAGINARY LOVESCAPES FOLDED HIS SORROWS IN AFRICAN DREAM WALKING PARKER HOME WHERE AFTERWARDS THEY WILL DANCE O CELESTIAL HOBO ON UNHOLY MISSIONS WITH BATTLE REPORTS AND BENEDICTIONS O BIRD WITH GRASS WINGS WHO STILL KNOWS EXACTLY WHERE HE IS HIGH ON LIFE SITTING ON THE CEILING AND WHO HAS SEEN THE WIND AND WOULD YOU WEAR HIS EYES WELL THEN HOLD YOUR BREASTS AND READ HIS TRUE-NORTH LEGEND WRIT ON LANDSCAPES OF LIFE IN MAPS OF AMERICA WHERE NIGHTINGALES STILL SOUND ON US AND THE SEARCH FOR ECSTASY NEVERTHELESS GOES ON

                                        FERLINGHETTI

Poems

I HAVE FOLDED MY SORROWS

I have folded my sorrows into the mantle of summer night,
Assigning each brief storm its allotted space in time,
Quietly pursuing catastrophic histories buried in my eyes.
And yes, the world is not some unplayed Cosmic Game,
And the sun is still ninety-three million miles from me,
And in the imaginary forest, the shingled hippo becomes
      the gay unicorn.
No, my traffic is not with addled keepers of yesterday's
      disasters,
Seekers of manifest disembowelment on shafts of yesterday's
      pains.
Blues come dressed like introspective echoes of a journey.
And yes, I have searched the rooms of the moon on cold
      summer nights.
And yes, I have refought those unfinished encounters.
      Still, they remain unfinished.
And yes, I have at times wished myself something different.

The tragedies are sung nightly at the funerals of the poet;
The revisited soul is wrapped in the aura of familiarity.

AFRICAN DREAM

In black core of night, it explodes
Silver thunder, rolling back my brain,
Bursting copper screens, memory worlds
Deep in star-fed beds of time,
Seducing my soul to diamond fires of night.
Faint outline, a ship—momentary fright
Lifted on waves of color,
Sunk in pits of light,
Drummed back through time,
Hummed back through mind,
Drumming, cracking the night.
Strange forest songs, skin sounds
Crashing through—no longer strange.
Incestuous yellow flowers tearing
Magic from the earth.
Moon-dipped rituals, led
By a scarlet god,
Caressed by ebony maidens
With daylight eyes,
Purple garments,
Noses that twitch,
Singing young girl songs
Of an ancient love
In dark, sunless places
Where memories are sealed,
Burned in eyes of tigers.

Suddenly wise, I fight the dream:
Green screams enfold my night.

WALKING PARKER HOME

Sweet beats of jazz impaled on slivers of wind
Kansas Black Morning/ First Horn Eyes/
Historical sound pictures on New Bird wings
People shouts/ boy alto dreams/Tomorrow's
Gold belled pipe of stops and future Blues Times
Lurking Hawkins/ shadows of Lester/ realization
Bronze fingers—brain extensions seeking trapped sounds
Ghetto thoughts/ bandstand courage/ solo flight
Nerve-wracked suspicions of newer songs and doubts
New York altar city/ black tears/ secret disciples
Hammer horn pounding soul marks on unswinging gates
Culture gods/ mob sounds/ visions of spikes
Panic excursions to tribal Jazz wombs and transfusions
Heroin nights of birth/ and soaring/ over boppy new ground.
Smothered rage covering pyramids of notes spontaneously
        exploding
Cool revelations/ shrill hopes/ beauty speared into
        greedy ears
Birdland nights on bop mountains, windy saxophone
        revolutions
Dayrooms of junk/ and melting walls and circling vultures/
Money cancer/ remembered pain/ terror flights/
Death and indestructible existence

In that Jazz corner of life
Wrapped in a mist of sound
His legacy, our Jazz-tinted dawn
Wailing his triumphs of oddly begotten dreams
Inviting the nerveless to feel once more
That fierce dying of humans consumed
In raging fires of Love.

5

AFTERWARDS, THEY SHALL DANCE

In the city of St. Francis they have taken down the statue of
     St. Francis,
And the hummingbirds all fly forward to protest, humming
     feather poems.

Bodenheim denounced everyone and wrote. Bodenheim had
     no sweet marijuana dreams,
Patriotic muscateleer, did not die seriously, no poet love to
     end with, gone.

Dylan took the stone cat's nap at St. Vincent's, vaticaned
     beer, no defense;
That poem shouted from his nun-filled room, an insult to the
     brain, nerves,
Save now from Swansea, white horses, beer birds, snore
     poems, Wales-bird.

Billie Holiday got lost on the subway and stayed there
          forever,
Raised little peace-of-mind gardens in out of the way
          stations,
And will go on living in wrappers of jazz silence forever,
     loved.

My face feels like a living emotional relief map, forever wet.
My hair is curling in anticipation of my own wild gardening.

Poor Edgar Allan Poe died translated, in unpressed pants,
     ended in light,
Surrounded by ecstatic gold bugs, his hegira blessed
     by Baudelaire's orgy.

Whether I am a poet or not, I use fifty dollars' worth
          of air every day, cool.
In order to exist I hide behind stacks of red and blue poems
And open little sensuous parasols, singing the nail-in-
          the-foot song, drinking cool beatitudes.

CELESTIAL HOBO

For every remembered dream
There are twenty nighttime lifetimes.

Under multiplied arcs of sleep
Zombie existences become Existence.

In night's warped rectangles
Stormy bathtubs of wavy sex
Come hotly drawn.

Everyday, confused in desperate poses,
Loses its hue, to Dada prodigies of black.
There never was a night that ended
Or began.

BATTLE REPORT

One thousand saxophones infiltrate the city,
Each with a man inside,
Hidden in ordinary cases,
Labeled FRAGILE.

A fleet of trumpets drops their hooks,
Inside at the outside.

Ten waves of trombones approach the city
Under blue cover
Of late autumn's neo-classical clouds.

Five hundred bassmen, all string feet tall,
Beating it back to the bass.

One hundred drummers, each a stick in each hand,
The delicate rumble of pianos, moving in.

The secret agent, an innocent bystander,
Drops a note in the wail box.

Five generals, gathered in the gallery,
Blowing plans.

At last, the secret code is flashed:
Now is the time, now is the time.

Attack: The sound of jazz.

The city falls.

BENEDICTION

Pale brown Moses went down to Egypt land
To let somebody's people go.
Keep him out of Florida, no UN there:
The poor governor is all alone,
With six hundred thousand illiterates.

America, I forgive you . . . I forgive you
Nailing black Jesus to an imported cross
Every six weeks in Dawson, Georgia.
America, I forgive you . . . I forgive you
Eating black children, I know your hunger.
America, I forgive you . . . I forgive you
Burning Japanese babies defensively—
I realize how necessary it was.
Your ancestor had beautiful thoughts in his brain.
His descendants are experts in real estate.
Your generals have mushrooming visions.
Every day your people get more and more
Cars, televisions, sickness, death dreams.
You must have been great
Alive.

UNHOLY MISSIONS

I want to be buried in an anonymous crater inside the moon.

I want to build miniature golf courses on all the stars.

I want to prove that Atlantis was a summer resort for cave men.

I want to prove that Los Angeles is a practical joke played on us by superior beings on a humorous planet.

I want to expose Heaven as an exclusive sanitarium filled with rich psychopaths who think they can fly.

I want to show that the Bible was serialized in a Roman children's magazine.

I want to prove that the sun was born when God fell asleep with a lit cigarette, tired after a hard night of judging.

I want to prove once and for all that I am not crazy.

WEST COAST SOUNDS — 1956

San Fran, hipster land,
Jazz sounds, wig sounds,
Earthquake sounds, others,
Allen on Chestnut Street,
Giving poetry to squares,
Corso on knees, pleading,
God eyes.
Rexroth, Ferlinghetti,
Swinging, in cellars,
Kerouac at Locke's,
Writing Neil
On high typewriter,
Neil, booting a choo-choo,
On zigzag tracks.
Now, many cats
Falling in,
New York cats,
Too many cats,
Monterey scene cooler,
San Franers, falling down.
Canneries closing.
Sardines splitting
For Mexico.
Me too.

FRAGMENT

. . . All those dead movie stars, peanut-buttered forever,
Do they kiss famous horses on the nose?
Do they see all of the latest horror movies?
How do they like the exclusive tombs, renaissance
      mailboxes,
With Bela Lugosi moving around down there
In his capeman Agron suit, sleepless walker,
With his arms full of morphine, his eyes suggesting
Frozen seesaws in cold playgrounds of yesterday.
What came first? The chicken or the spike?
What came last? The needle or the haystack?
That scream was a rumor and remained unscreamed,
Unnoted among narcotic breakfasts and raving love fiends,
Sexy rides on Gothic streetcars and Buddha lost
      in a phone booth,
Cold talking wind-people, three-dimensional valentines,
Torn from magic tenements in the long Decembers of today.
Easter-faced skylarks, low-flying Mexican birds,
The oracle of the crickets ticking off jazz *Te Deums,*
Our Lady of Nicotine, madonna without child,
Releases her pale balloon, snatched from the folding year,
All the daring young headhunters, traumatic in inflammatory
      bathing suits,
Shriek grim fairy tales, while convenient needles fall
      out of haystacks.
Charlie Parker was a great electrician who went around
      wiring people.

GRANDFATHER WAS QUEER, TOO

He was first seen in a Louisiana bayou,
Playing chess with an intellectual lobster.
They burned his linoleum house alive
And sent that intellectual off to jail.
He wrote home every day, to no avail.
Grandfather had cut out, he couldn't raise the bail.

Next seen, skiing on some dusty Texas road,
An intellectual's soul hung from his ears,
Discussing politics with an unemployed butterfly.
They hung that poor butterfly, poor butterfly.
Grandfather had cut out, he couldn't raise the bail.

Next seen on the Arizona desert, walking,
Applying soothing poultices to the teeth
Of an aching mountain.
Dentists all over the state brought gauze balls,
Bandaged the mountain, buried it at sea.
Grandfather had cut out, he couldn't raise the bail.

Next seen in California, the top part,
Arranging a marriage, mating trees,
Crossing a rich redwood and a black pine.
He was exposed by the Boy Scouts of America.
The trees were arrested on a vag charge.
Grandfather cut out, he couldn't raise the bail.

Now I have seen him here. He is beat.
His girlfriend has green ears;
She is twenty-three months pregnant.
I kissed them both:
Live happily ever after.

13

BAGEL SHOP JAZZ

Shadow people, projected on coffee-shop walls.
Memory formed echoes of a generation past
Beating into now.

Nightfall creatures, eating each other
Over a noisy cup of coffee.

Mulberry-eyed girls in black stockings,
Smelling vaguely of mint jelly and last night's bongo
      drummer,
Making profound remarks on the shapes of navels,
Wondering how the short Sunset week
Became the long Grant Avenue night,
Love tinted, beat angels,
Doomed to see their coffee dreams
Crushed on the floors of time,
As they fling their arrow legs
To the heavens,
Losing their doubts in the beat.

Turtle-neck angel guys, black-haired dungaree guys,
Caesar-jawed, with synagogue eyes,
World travelers on the forty-one bus,
Mixing jazz with paint talk,
High rent, Bartok, classical murders,
The pot shortage and last night's bust.
Lost in a dream world,
Where time is told with a beat.

Coffee-faced Ivy Leaguers, in Cambridge jackets,
Whose personal Harvard was a Fillmore district step,
Weighted down with conga drums,
The ancestral cross, the Othello-laid curse,
Talking of Bird and Diz and Miles,
The secret terrible hurts,
Wrapped in cool hipster smiles,
Telling themselves, under the talk,
This shot must be the end,
Hoping the beat is really the truth.

The guilty police arrive.

Brief, beautiful shadows, burned on walls of night.

REFLECTIONS ON A SMALL PARADE

When I see the little Buddhist scouts
Marching with their Zen mothers
To tea ceremonies at the rock garden,
I shake my head. . . . It falls off.

HART . . . . CRANE

They fear you, Crane . . . . you whispered aloft, pains they
   buried forever . . . .

They hate you, Crane . . . . your sur-real eclipses blot out their
   muted sun . . . .

They miss you, Crane . . . . your footprints are on their rotting
   teeth . . . .

They need you, Crane . . . . their walking minds are worn to
   bony core . . . .

They want you, Crane . . . . stay hidden beneath shadowed
   bookstore tables . . . .

They call you, Crane . . . . they shout your name in deserted
   phonebooths . . . .

They beat you, Crane . . . . they draw your mouth on their
   lovers' bodies . . . .

They know you, Crane . . . . they have memorized the pimples
   on your soul . . . .

They seek you, Crane . . . . your face is on secret stamps
   pinned to hidden envelopes . . . .

They buy you, Crane . . . . your petrified sperm is treasured
   by marble lovers . . . .

They hear you, Crane . . . . you are screaming from their
   turned-off radios . . . .

They see you, Crane .... you are mirrored in black windows
on deserted streetcorners ....

They read you, Crane .... your books are opened in under-
ground libraries ....

They paint you, Crane .... your eyebrows are on their glossy
calendars ....

They teach you, Crane .... in secret huddles beneath football
stadiums ....

They sell you, Crane .... you are spreadeagled on grills
of poetic eating places ....

They celebrate you, Crane .... you are a sequined float
in clandestine beauty processions ....

They worship you, Crane .... you are enshrined on
suicide altars of pain ....

They kill you, Crane .... you are electrocuted at breakfast
in gas-chamber kitchens ....

They are relieved, Crane .... you have gone, taking your
realities with you ....

They deny you, Crane .... you are safely dead, but we know,
Crane, you never were ....

They live you, Crane .... ON THE BRIDGE.

EAST FIFTH STREET (N.Y.)

Twisting brass, key of G, tenement stoned,
Singing Jacob's song, with Caribbe emphasis.

Flinging the curls of infant rabbis, gently,
Into the glowing East Side night.

Esther's hand, in Malinche's clasped,
Traps the fly of evening, forever.

Ancient log-rolling caps of Caribbe waves
Splashing crowded harbors of endless steps.

Angry, fire-eyed children clutch transient winds,
Singing Gypsy songs, love me now, love me now.

The echoes return, riding the voice of the river,
As time cries out, on the skin of an African drum.

BIRD WITH PAINTED WINGS

Monet whispered softly,
Drowned love
In pools of light.

Picasso shouted nightmares,
Screaming: Climb inside yourself,
There is a madness there.

Braque gave the echo, precisely.

Mondrian exposed squares.

As the Mexicans roared
In the star-torn Indian night,
Fire lifted Paricutin,
Springing red from black earth.

Modigliani, naked, exposed sadness.

Degas exposed angels in ballet skins,
Smoked behind walls of Marseilles' absinthe dens.

Kollwitz served tears in wooden spoons,
Under dark moons, forever sorrowed.

Rousseau shouted poetry
From his window on that mad world.

A burning bird whistled on high:
Eat it all,
Die!

BLUES NOTE

Ray Charles is the black wind of Kilimanjaro,
Screaming up-and-down blues,
Moaning happy on all the elevators of my time.

Smiling into the camera, with an African symphony
Hidden in his throat, and (*I Got a Woman*) wails, too.

He burst from Bessie's crushed black skull
One cold night outside of Nashville, shouting,
And grows bluer from memory, glowing bluer, still.

At certain times you can see the moon
Balanced on his head.

From his mouth he hurls chunks of raw soul.
He separated the sea of polluted sounds
And led the blues into the Promised Land.

Ray Charles is a dangerous man ('way cross town),
And I love him.

for Ray Charles's birthday
N.Y.C. / 1961

DEAR JOHN:

It has been a lifetime, it seems.
I am no longer what I once was,
So I can't speak with my old eloquence.
I have become less and darker
Than a shadow. Sometimes I think
I've never recovered from Danny's party;
You remember that bash, don't you?

I don't know what happened or when,
But I don't make that scene anymore.
So I just sit here in that new,
Fluorescent lighting, feeling strange
As an old deserted movie set.

There isn't much to do around here
Anymore, so I just sit around,
Thinking about you and Doc and
Those crazy-beauty whores we loved.

I often wonder how Doc would smile
About the lab being turned into a club
Of people; I guess he'd want to bottle a few, for study;
He was crazy enough to do that, you know.

Not much more to say. We've got a media agency,
Whatever that is, two big fashionable eating joints,
For Carmel people and tourists, and a coupla' gift joints.
Only time anything happens is when those poor dreamers
Come down from S.F., but the rents won't let them stay.
Well, so long for now. Here come a coupla' paisans
Trying out their new Buick. All that gas bugs me.

Yours in warm remembrance,

Cannery Row

PLEA

Voyager, wanderer of the heart,
Off to
      a million midnights, black, black,
Voyager, wanderer of star worlds,
Off to
      a million tomorrows, black, black,
Seek and find Hiroshima's children,
      Send them back, send them back.
Tear open concrete-sealed cathedrals, spiritually locked,
      Fill vacant theaters with their musty diversions,
      Almost forgotten laughter.

Give us back the twisted sons
Poisoned by mildewed fathers.
Find again the used-up whores,
Dying in some forgotten corner,
Find sunlight, and barking dogs,
For the lost, decayed in sorry jails.
Find pity, find Hell for wax bitches,
Hidden in the bowels of male Cadillacs.
Find tomorrow and nexttime for Negro millionaires
Hopelessly trapped in their luxurious complexions.
Find love, and an everlasting fix for hopeless junkies,
Stealing into lost night, long time.

Voyager now,
            Off to a million midnights, black, black,
Seek and find Hiroshima's children,
            Send them back, send them back.

GINSBERG (for Allen)

Ginsberg won't stop tossing lions to the martyrs.
This ends the campaign by leftwing cardinals to elect
    an Eskimo Pope.
The Church is becoming alarmed by the number of people
    defecting to God.
The Holy Intelligence Agency is puzzled: they have proof
    he is broke and his agents
Use spiritual brainwashing in addition to promises
    of quick sainthood.
The holy stepfather cautioned the faithful to emulate none of
    the saints who hide behind the Fifth Commandment
    when persecuted.
There is also a move to cut off Ginsberg's supply of lions.
The poet continues to smoke carnal knowledge knowingly.
I am sure the government can't prove that he is
    stolen property;
I have proof that he was Gertrude Stein's medicine chest.
I am not not an I, secret wick, I do nothing,
    light myself, burn.
Allen passed through that Black Hole of Calcutta
    behind my eyes;
He was wearing rings and hoops of longitude and latitude.
He must have been hurt by real love, and false love, too.
He can cling and fall and clasp eyes with the best,
Design exciting families with no people in them,
Stuffed with bleeding expressions of human form.
Why I love him, though, is equatorially sound:
I love him because his eyes leak.

HOLLYWOOD

Five square miles of ultra-contemporary nymphomania,
Two dozen homos, to every sapiens, at last countdown,
Ugly Plymouths, swapping exhaust with red convertible
    Buicks,
Twelve-year-old mothers suing for child support,
Secondhand radios making it with wide-screen TV sets,
Unhustling junkies shooting mothball fixes, insect junk,
Unemployed pimps living on neon backs of
Unemployed whores.

Bisexual traffic lights, red-faced, with green shades,
Fastest guns in video West slinging lisps with slowest fairies
    in ivy East,
Unlit starlets seeking an unfilled galaxy, with an opening,
Ranch Market hipsters who lost their cool in gradeschool,
Yesterday idols, idle, whose faces were made of clay.

Horrible movie-makers making horrors that move,
Teenage, were-kids, hot-rockers, rolling with the blows,
Successful screen writers drinking down unsuccessful screams,
Plastic beatniks in pubic beards, with artistically dirtied
    feet,
Recreated Jimmy Deans, pompadours looking for sports-car
    mothers,
Sunset strippers, clothed to the hilt—and no further.

San Francisco poets looking for an out place, looking way
          out of place,
Televised detectives getting waves from television defectives,
Disc jockeys with all-night shows and all-day habits,
Bored Fords, with nothing in their future but grease jobs,
Hindu holymen with police records clear back to Alabama,
Mondrian-faced drive-ins featuring hamburger-broiled
          charcoal
Served in laminated fortune cookies.

Channel Something piano players down to their last mom,
Down-at-head pot-smokers with down-at-heel eyes,
Death-faced agents living on ten percent of nothing,
Lady painters with three names having one-man shows
          of expensive framing,
Unemployed Broadway actors with nothing to offer but talent
          trying to look stupid,

In-group sick comedians, a lot sicker than their comedy,
          REAL SICK,
No coast jazz musicians uncommitted, waiting to be
          committed,
Scoopy columnists with two punctuation marks, both periods,
Native-son Woodmen of the West, utterly convinced
          that Donald Duck is Jewish,
Legions of decency borrowing their decency from the Legion,
Impatient Cadillacs trading in their owners
          for more successful models,

Lanky Calypso singers, caught with their fads down,
      trapped in beat coffee cups
With small-chested actresses, bosomed out
      by the big breast scene,
Unsympathetic dope-peddlers, who refuse to honor credit
      cards,
Carping critics refusing to see what's good,
      just because it isn't present,
Lonely old De Mille-divorced God, seeking a new producer
With a couple of rebuilt commandments . . .
Hollywood I salute you, artistic cancer of the universe!

SESSION TONGUES

Lost wax process, ear-wax out using vortex from planetarium
      so
New kind Greek, written more often than hurricanes,
      in afternoon,
Put it with the whip, or the fear of something or nothing
      soon.
Take new glowing onion and replace in ice-cube tray,
      glowing too,
Melt in sun at one million degrees and shape into fish,
      glowing
In radiation seas and strange unnoticed sensation, death.

MINGUS

String-chewing bass players,
Plucking rolled balls of sound
From the jazz-scented night.

Feeding hungry beat seekers
Finger-shaped heartbeats,
Driving ivory nails
Into their greedy eyes.

Smoke crystals, from the nostrils
Of released jazz demons,
Crash from foggy yesterday
To the light
Of imaginary night.

I, TOO, KNOW WHAT I AM NOT

No, I am not death wishes of sacred rapists, singing
      on candy gallows.
No, I am not spoor of Creole murderers hiding
      in crepe-paper bayous.
No, I am not yells of some assassinated inventor, locked
      in his burning machine.
No, I am not forced breathing of Cairo's senile burglar,
      in lead shoes.
No, I am not Indian-summer fruit of Negro piano tuners,
      with muslin gloves.
No, I am not noise of two-gun senators, in hallowed
      peppermint hall.
No, I am not pipe-smoke hopes of cynical chiropractors,
      traffickers in illegal bone.
No, I am not pitchblende curse of Indian suicides,
      in bonnets of flaming water.
No, I am not soap-powder sighs of impotent window washers,
      in pants of air.
No, I am not kisses of tubercular sun addicts, smiling
      through rayon lips.
No, I am not chipped philosopher's tattered ideas sunk
      in his granite brain.
No, I am not cry of amethyst heron, winged stone in flight
      from cambric bullets.
No, I am not sting of the neurotic bee, frustrated
      in cheesecloth gardens.
No, I am not peal of muted bell, clapperless
      in the faded glory.
No, I am not report of silenced guns, helpless
      in the pacifist hands.
No, I am not call of wounded hunter, alone
      in the forest of bone.

No, I am not eyes of the infant owls hatching
    the roofless night.
No, I am not the whistle of Havana whores with cribs
    of Cuban death.
No, I am not shriek of Bantu children, bent
    under pennywhistle whips.
No, I am not whisper of the African trees,
    leafy Congo telephones.
No, I am not Leadbelly of blues, escaped from guitar jails.
No, I am not anything that is anything I am not.

HIGH ON LIFE

    Floating on superficially elevated streets
secretly nude,
    Subtle forked tongues of sensuous fog
probe and core
    Deliciously into my chapped-lipped pores
coolly whistling,
    Spiraling in hollowed caves of skin-stretched me,
totally doorless,
    Emptied of vital parts, previously evicted finally
by landlord mind
    To make nerve-lined living space, needed desperately
by my transient, sightless, sleepless,
    Soul.

DOLOROUS ECHO

The holey little holes
In my skin,
Millions of little
Secret graves,
Filled with dead
Feelings
That won't stay
Dead.

The hairy little hairs
On my head,
Millions of little
Secret trees,
Filled with dead
Birds,
That won't stay
Dead.

When I die,
I won't stay
Dead.

SAN FRANCISCO BEAT

Hidden in the eye of jazz,
Secretly balling, against time
I see cabbage eye, malignant successes,
Eating plastic ball-shaped benzedrines,
Hiding in the windows of empty doghouses,
Among limb shops, selling breast,
To rookie policemen.

Jazz cops with ivory nightsticks,
Leaning on the heads of imitation Negroes,
Selling ice cubes to returned virgins,
Wrapping velvet Band-aids, over holes
In the arms of heaven-headed junkies.

Hawkeyed baggy-pants businessmen,
Building earthquake-proof, aluminum whorehouses,
Guaranteeing satisfaction to pinstripe murderers,
Or your money back to West Heaven,
Full of glorious, Caesarean-section politicians,
Giving kisses to round half-lipped babies,
Eating metal jazz, from cavities, in father's chest,
Purchased in flagpole war, to leave balloon-chested
Unfreaked Reader's Digest women grinning at Coit Tower.

Dripping harmless flagellations on the scaly backs
Of graduate celibates selling polka-dot diaphragms
To gay young monsters drowning in flowing gutters
Of timely discussions on telemothervisionfather,
Gradually sucking the heads of littlesmallbig people,
Into cathode obedience, demanding all onions
For one flyspeck of love I keep hidden,
In my webbed feet,
Out of Step.

JAZZ *TE DEUM* FOR INHALING
AT MEXICAN BONFIRES

Let us write reeling sagas about heroic movie stars who failed
and lived.

Let us poetize on twelve-tone prints of Schoenberg and naked
office girls.

Let us compose Teutonic folksongs on the death of Israel's
German tribe.

Let us chant those thousand choruses of Nefertiti's funeral
and desert grief festivals.

Let us pluck lion-gut strings of marble lutes on teak decks
of Ming junks.

Let us walk through bloody Florentine gates using secret
Medici keys.

Let us splash in Persian swimming pools among floating shahs
and dead concubines.

Let us wear robes of legendary eunuchs for lovemaking
with lewd statues.

Let us wear flaming hats to Mongol dances on mummified
khans' sacred Gobi.

Let us smoke petrified bamboo shoots in cool waiting rooms
of Angkor Wat.

Let us wear suttee memories of Bengal widows on holy
Ganges' burning ghats.

Let us inhale dreamy eternities from alabaster pipes and sail
glowing solar boats.

Let us walk naked in radiant glacial rains and cool morphic
thunderstorms.

Let us shrink into pygmy bo trees and cast holy shadows
on melted cities.

Let us read forbidden Sanskrit on lotus mounds
of Buddhist nuns.

Let us imitate Homeric Trojans on sea-girt beds
    of Delphic whorehouses.
Let us sing illegal requiems on execution sabbaths
    of sexy Popes and pray.
Let us wail circumsion Jossanas of lost Samaritans buried
    in rumors of love.
Let us carry Inca staves to hawk-priest rituals on altars
    of bleeding suns.
Let us blow African jazz in Alabama jungles and wail
    savage lovesongs of unchained fire.
Let us melt jelly-like into damp caves of lip-biting women
    and feel dew-charred dampnesses of gyrating
    universes of smoke-flavored jazz.

LADIES

How many ladies in how many paintings
Escaped how many snakes?

How many snakes in how many paintings
Escaped how many ladies?

Every lady escaped, but one.
Not one goddam snake ever escaped.

It's a hell of a lot safer
To be a lady
Than a snake.

SONG OF THE BROKEN GIRAFFE

I have heard the song of the broken giraffe, and sung it. . . .
The frozen sun has browned me to a rumor and slanted my
    navel.
I have consorted with vulgar crocodiles on banks
    of lewd rivers.
Yes, it is true, God has become mad, from centuries
    of frustration.
When I think of all the girls I never made love to,
    I am shocked.
Every time they elect me President, I hide in the bathroom.
When you come, bring me a tourniquet for our wounded
    moon.
In an emergency, I can rearrange your beautiful wreckage
With broken giraffe demolitions and lovely colorless
    explosions.
Come, you sexy Ferris wheel, ignore my illustrated
    bathing suit.
Don't laugh at my ignorance, I may be a great
    bullfighter, olé!
I wanted to compose a great mass, but I couldn't kneel
    properly.
Yes, they did tempt me with airplanes, but I wouldn't bite,
    no sir-ee.
Unable to avoid hospitals, I still refused to become a doctor.
They continued to throw reason, but I failed
    in the clutch again.
It's true, I no longer use my family as a frame of reference.
The clothing they gave me was smart but no good
    for train wrecks.

I continued to love despite all the traffic-light difficulties.
In most cases, a sane hermit will beat a good big man.
We waited in vain for the forest fire, but the bus was late.
All night we baked the government into a big mud pie.
Not one century passed without Shakespeare calling us
      dirty names.
With all those syllables, we couldn't write a cheerful
      death notice.
The man said we could have a birthday party if we
      surrendered.
Their soldiers refused to wear evening gowns on guard duty.
Those men in the basement are former breakfast-food
      salesmen.
We had a choice of fantasies, but naturally we were greedy.
If they leave me alone, I will become a fallen-leaf tycoon.
Maybe Peter Rabbit will forgive us our trespasses;
      one never knows.
At the moment of truth we were dancing a minuet and
      missed out.
After the nuns went home, the Pope threw a big masquerade
      ball.
When the hemlock turned rancid, I returned the cup at once,
      yes sir-ee.
Hurry, the barometer's falling; bring a storm before
      it's too late.
We shall reserve evenings for murder or television,
      whichever is convenient.
Yes, beyond a shadow of a doubt, Rumpelstiltskin
      was emotionally disturbed.

VOYAGERS

Black leather angels of
Pop-bopping stallions searching
In the corners of peace
For violence
That exists
Deep in their
Own sexless breasts,
Creeping away into highway dark,
To find spark-born oblivion
Among the debris of wrecked motorcycles,
Strips of torn metal eagles
Hanging from frames,
Of good-life daddies, transporting
Children's remains
To worn out art corners,
Concealed among the announcements
Of poetry sessions,
Filtering through jazz readings,
Seeking a lost intestine,
Removed by
Good daddy doctor
That day they were
Paroled from their
Mama's belly.
Death's billboard painters
Making gigantic caricatures
Of life,
Minute sounds of belching,
In the backyards of silence,
Betrayed into shouting,
Spotlighting their hiding places,
Revealing cherished murders
To uncaring nonchalant policemen,
Too busy birdwatching

Squares of concrete
To notice the public bleedings
On four o'clock streetcorners.
Flowing on the shadow-tread streets,
In shoulder-bumping walktime,
The garrulous street lamps
Report rattlings to each other's
Splintered-wood poems,
Printed on the lost noise
Of dead traffic.
The aging forest is burning itself,
Phoenixlike reborn,
The bush and trees of glass
Silhouette crisply burning stars,
The green glass body
Of phantom women,
Composed of airs of night,
Presses me deeply, crying
Between ruby-quartz thighs,
Neon sperm glows
At the tip,
My poem
Spurting at the thrust
Into tomorrow.

II

Twice-maimed shrews, ailing
In elongated slots
Of pubic splendor
Engulfed by luxurious dogs,
Sniffing curiously,
Among alcohol asylums,
Populated by oversexed
Poverty-stricken brainstorms,
Puberty-stunned explosions

Raging in and out of insane comas,
Spouting word fountains
At the shriveled mouths
Of wildly depraved roses
As Cassandra dances
On the singed eyelids
Of sleepless ants.

Flapping plaid tongues poked
From dying normality faces
Poised to scoop out the
Dirt-filled navels
Of whores and poets
Concealed inside unexploded bodies
Of defective firecrackers, dreaming
Secretly of blowing up
In the face of Time.

III

Be aware of being aware, of been aware,
Of the day the sky cracked up, raining private rain
Inside the heads of circling cats, snapping
Brittle vertebrae, kicking the reality drag.

God, you are
A big black pot
Full of torn handkerchiefs
Mixed with secondhand
Definitions.

IV

Muted explosions in unbowed plastic heads
Of psychotic chessmen illuminate illusions
Held by faint flowing hands, holding

Cut-glass bowls of trapped eyes,
Sprawled among wispy pot-smoke ceilings
Of superimposed accusations;
Punctuated by hooked coughing
Of watery clowns, consecrated idiots,
Sleepy-eyed Christ, aborted Marys.

V

Cynical jazz, blasted from neon intestines,
Electrically had by departed saxophone maniacs,
Noisy artfully contrived screams,
Presenceless souls, trapped
On thin anonymous discs of eroded wax,
Continuous shrieks spearing through
Marbleskin earshaped antennae
Of aesthetic-soaked pincushions,
Springfoot leapers, frozen in flight,
Clinging to shallow bowled spoons,
Twisting in desperately clawed caves
Holding pinkish moisture, dripped
By parched secret needle-sucking mouths
Brooding on stoned cliffs of tarnished arms.
Overlooking underlooking innerlooking
Hysterically conceived combinations,
Of eyes and mother genitals,
Auto-sculpted into ecstatic images
Of long-loved cherished pain.
Digging among reddened lipstained cups,
Of leftover sadness,
Hopelessly hoping hopefully
To find love
Of a dead moon
Or a poem.

WOULD YOU WEAR MY EYES?

My body is a torn mattress,
Disheveled throbbing place
For the comings and goings
Of loveless transients.
The whole of me
Is an unfurnished room
Filled with dank breath
Escaping in gasps to nowhere.
Before completely objective mirrors
I have shot myself with my eyes,
But death refused my advances.
I have walked on my walls each night
Through strange landscapes in my head.
I have brushed my teeth with orange peel,
Iced with cold blood from the dripping faucets.
My face is covered with maps of dead nations;
My hair is littered with drying ragweed.
Bitter raisins drip haphazardly from my nostrils
While schools of glowing minnows swim from my mouth.
The nipples of my breasts are sun-browned cockleburrs;
Long-forgotten Indian tribes fight battles on my chest
Unaware of the sunken ships rotting in my stomach.
My legs are charred remains of burned cypress trees;
My feet are covered with moss from bayous, flowing
          across my floor.
I can't go out anymore.
I shall sit on my ceiling.
Would you wear my eyes?

MATRICULATION

Big naked professors, standing out in the cold, weary
(that whip festival brings it out, the young more so).

Last year's cotillion instructors with blackjacks and cookies
(refreshments are important when things are slow, you
        know).

Brawny swimming instructors quivering on canvas
        life-saving stretchers
(protection of the young is the duty of every orgy-master).

Kilted piano players playing suggestive minuets on gaily
        decorated triangles
(the music should build to the climax then explode
        like overloaded creampuffs).

Skinny porters dusting off the heaving bodies with velvet
        cactus leaves
(the period just after fertilization is important
        to the victim's future).

SULLEN BAKERIES OF TOTAL RECALL

Sometimes I feel the ones who escaped the ovens where
    Germans shall forever cook their spiritual meals are
    leaning against my eyes.

A wounded margolis in his suit of horror, his eyes of elevated
    Brownsville, that taste of gas in his smile, I could hear
    it when my ears were Mexican weed.

My first reaction is to be angry with Moses for not commit-
    ting suicide; my second reaction is to be furious with
    the Germans for not committing suicide; my third
    reaction is one of total disappointment for not commit-
    ting suicide. I think of Chaplin and roll a mental
    cigarette. I slowly remove my bayonet, write a poem
    about a poetic poem, dedicated to the Aleutian Islands.

The bony oboe doorway beyond the burning nose translates
    me into Hebrew. I know that Faust was actually anti-
    symbolic and would never have married Kate Smith.

And how many Ophelias escaped from Ruth's letter? Are
    teenage cancellations out? . . . Here, here's my brain
    receipt, take my skin check, I want Juliet on the hoof.
    Because of what happened, sex is holy by virtue of
    arithmetic and welcome dampness.

Someone hurled an eyelid at the moon. . . . My shadow
    wanders off, lost in black sidestreets, vulnerable to the
    cooling soft switchblade of light blinking: DONT WALK.
    . . . Green. . . . My footsteps follow me at a distance.

I acknowledge the demands of Surrealist realization. I challenge Apollinaire to stagger drunk from his grave and write a poem about the Rosenbergs' last days in a housing project, how Salvator Agron spread his cape for one last snapshot of Jesus speeding through Puerto Rico, his car radio blasting, mowing down the tilting Hiltons, speeding to the voltage mass of St. Sing Sing, the famous gothic burning ghats on the banks of the sacred Hudson. . . . And yet when I think of those ovens, I turn my head in any other direction.

I am doing my best to dry my mind. The brain's a bully. I go to hospitals named after sadists with diseases that don't exist and demand famous operations that Dr. Schweitzer hasn't invented yet; they give me drugs while I wait for Albert to emerge from the jungle: his wise organ music may remove this malingering sensitivity before it infects my other organs.

The rabbi across the table from me is also a firm believer in suicide. He wanted to be an actor on Second Avenue and eat dinner across from the theater and be insecure and marry an Adler and talk about Peretz and Aleichem and Secunda, and wake up to find himself with an important role in an established theater. He is holy and eats very little and reads like a scholar and wants to kill himself. I refuse to tell him the time. If necessary, I will write the script and we will go together.

A REMEMBERED BEAT

We heard our beat faintly then,
When John Hoffman hitchhiked with enemy gods
And died in Mexicans' land,
Choked on his dreams of blood and love,
Leaving his poems on dark other side of time,
And first slight hint of a beat.

When Parker, a poet in jazz,
Gave one hundred seventy pounds to a one-ounce needle,
His music, his life,
Six hipsters from uptown
Called it a religious sacrifice
And wore turbans.
Our poet wore lonely death,
Leaving his breath in a beat.

We remember when Max Bodenheim remembered Lorca
And challenged death nightly, with a port pint
Full of mixed-up crazy love and thirty years' bitter
Memory in poet life,
Only to end as hero of a slaughter poem
Written by a maniac, on a Third Avenue night of hell,
And we were there, lost in the sound of a beat.

We remember thin cafeteria Sanskrit scholars
Reading old telephone directories aloud,
Trying to find Buddha or Truth
Among columns of private detectives, private sanitariums
And committees for rehabilitation of bisexual Eskimos,
And the unlisted trace of a beat.

We remember when poets removed tangled brains
To save for a saner time,
When organization men in pink ties declared television love,
Opening the age of electrical stone
As all do-gooders shouted: Punch time clocks,
Or your neighbors, or your youngest boy,
While a warload of young poets
Perished in Pusan's swamp,
Drowned in a flood of matchbook covers from home.
Survivors hid themselves in the folds of a cocaine
        nighttime robe,
As pill time stretched across white powdered deserts
And roots of exotic cactus bloomed in caves of the mind,
As nirvana came dancing, prancing in time to the beat,
Leading new ways through friend-filled narcotic graveyards
To hidden Pacific, big hell, quiet peace of Big Sur
Where that proud pornographer smiles on a redwood throne
As birds pound the air with a beat.

PATRIOTIC ODE ON THE FOURTEENTH ANNIVERSARY OF THE PERSECUTION OF CHARLIE CHAPLIN

Come on out of there with your hands up, Chaplin,
In your Sitting Bull suit, with your amazing new Presto
        Lighter.
We caught you. We found your fingerprints on the World's
        Fair.
Give us back the money and start over as a cowboy.
Come on, Chaplin, we mean business.

CAMUS: I WANT TO KNOW

Camus, I want to know, does the cold knife of wind plunge
    noiselessly into the soul, finally

Camus, I want to know, does the seated death wing as sud-
    den, swifter than leaden Fascist bullets . . .

Camus, sand-faced rebel from Olympus, brain lit, shining
    cleanly, on far historical peaks . . .

Camus, I want to know, does the jagged fender resemble
    Franco, standing spiked at Madrid's Goyaesque
    wound

Camus, I want to know, the dull aesthetics, rubbery thump of
    exploding wheels, the tick-pock of dust on steel

Camus, I want to know, does it clackety clack like that destiny
    train, shrieking to the Finland station

Camus, I want to know, does the sorrowful cry of unwilling
    companions console the dying air . . .

Camus, I want to know, does the cry of protested death sing,
    like binding vow of lovers' nod

Camus, I want to know, does the bitter taste of jagged glass
    sweeten the ripped tongue, dried

Camus, I want to know, does the sour taste of unfulfilled
    promise flee the dying mouth and eyes and lip

Camus, I want to know, does the liberated blood bubble hotly
    to the soil, microscopic Red Seas

Camus, I want to know, does the cyclop headlight illuminate
nerve-lined pits of final desires

Camus, I want to know, does the secret hoard of unanswered
queries scream for ultimate solutions

Camus, I want to know, does the eye of time blink in antici-
pation of recaptured seasons enriched

Camus, I want to know, does the sliver of quartz sensoulize
the clash of flesh on chrome and bone

Camus, I want to know, does the piercing spear of death
imitate denied desire, internal crucifixion

Camus, I want to know, does the spiritual juice flee as slowly,
as the Saharablood of prophets' sons

Camus, I want to know, does it mirror the Arab virgin, her
sex impaled on some soldier's wine bottle

Camus, I shall follow you over itching floors of black deserts,
across roofs of burning palms . . .

Camus, I shall crawl on sandpaper knees on oasis bottoms of
secret Bedouin wells, cursing . . .

Camus, I shall reach the hot sky, my brown mouth filled with
fragile telephones, sans rings . . .

Camus, I shall mumble long-cherished gibberish through
layers of protesting heat, demanding . . .

Camus, I shall scream but one awesome question, does *death
exist? Camus, I want to know . . .*

TO MY SON PARKER,
ASLEEP IN THE NEXT ROOM

On ochre walls in ice-formed caves shaggy Neanderthals
    marked their place in time.
On germinal trees in equatorial stands embryonic giants
    carved beginnings.
On Tasmanian flatlands mud-clothed first men hacked rock,
    still soft.
On Melanesian mountain peaks barked heads were reared
    in pride and beauty.
On steamy Java's cooling lava stooped humans raised stones
    to altar height.
On newborn China's plain mythless sons of Han acquired
    peaked gods with teak faces.
On holy India's sacred soil future gods carved worshipped
    reflections.
On Coptic Ethiopia's pimple rock pyramid builders tore
    volcanoes from earth.
On death-loving Egypt's godly sands living sacrifices carved
    naked power.
On Sumeria's cliffs speechless artists gouged messages
    to men yet uncreated.
On glorious Assyria's earthen dens art priests chipped
    figures of awe and hidden dimensions.
On splendored Peru's gold-stained body filigreed temples
    were torn from severed hands.
On perfect Greece's bloody sites marble stirred
    under hands of men.
On degenerate Rome's trembling sod imitators sculpted lies
    into beauty.

On slave Europe's prostrate form chained souls shaped free
men.
On wild America's green torso original men painted
glacial languages.
On cold Arctica's snowy surface leathery men raised totems
in frozen air.
On this shore, you are all men, before, forever, eternally
free in all things.
On this shore, we shall raise our monuments of stones,
of wood, of mud, of color, of labor, of belief, of being,
of life, of love, of self, of man expressed
in self-determined compliance, or willful revolt,
secure in this avowed truth, that no man is our master,
nor can any ever be, at any time in time to come.

CINCOPHRENICPOET

A cincophrenic poet called
a meeting of all five of
him at which four of the
most powerful of him voted
to expel the weakest of him
who didn't dig it, coughing
poetry for revenge, beseech-
ing all horizontal reserves
to cross, spiral, and whirl.

TEEVEE PEOPLE

Assuming the posture of frogs, croaking at appointed times,
Loudly treading the plastic floors of copied temples,
The creeping cardboard creatures, endlessly creeping,
In and out of time, eating the clock by the hour,
Poets of the gray universities in history suits,
Dripping false Greek dirges from tweedy beards,
While all the Troys are consumed in mushroom clouds.

The younger machines occupy miles of dark benches,
Enjoying self-induced vacations of the mind,
Eating textbook rinds, spitting culture seeds,
Dreaming an exotic name to give their latest defeat,
Computing the hours on computer minds.

The cold land breathes death rattles, trembling,
The dark sky casts shadows across the wounds
Beneath the bright clothing of well-fed machines,
The hungry heart inside the hungry hearts,
Beats silently, beats softly, beats, beats.

THE EYES TOO

My eyes too have souls that rage
At the sight of butterflies walking,
At the crime of a ship cutting an ocean in two,
At visions of girls who should be naked
Sitting at lunch counters eyeballing newspapers,
At complacent faces of staring clocks
Objectively canceling lives
With ticks.

THE DAY AFTER

Was the day six Hindu holymen
        tore up their sweepstakes tickets.

Was the day six movie stars
        removed their freak suits, disappeared.

Was the day six senile generals
        removed their prostates, reappeared.

Was the day six juvenile delinquents
        removed their brass knuckles, masturbated.

Was the day six shells of burned-out bodies of Hiroshima's
        children crawled across petrified oceans,
        dragging crates of burning philosophies
          over indignant civilized mountain ranges,
        weaved caterpillary among deserted Vaticans,
        paused to take pictures of hollow White Houses,
          wakened sleeping Zhivagos in silent Kremlins.

Was the day six sharkskin-suited oracles
        caused six certified public accountants
          to decide for Christ at the boxing arena.

WAR MEMOIR

Jazz—listen to it at your own risk.
At the beginning, a warm dark place.

(Her screams were trumpet laughter,
Not quite blues, but almost sinful.)

Crying above the pain, we forgave ourselves;
Original sin seemed a broken record.
God played blues to kill time, all the time.
Red-waved rivers floated us into life.

(So much laughter, concealed by blood and faith;
Life is a saxophone played by death.)

Greedy to please, we learned to cry;
Hungry to live, we learned to die.
The heart is a sad musician,
Forever playing the blues.

The blues blow life, as life blows fright;
Death begins, jazz blows soft in the night,
Too soft for ears of men whose minds
Hear only the sound of death, of war,
Of flagwrapped cremation in bitter lands.

No chords of jazz as mud is shoveled
Into the mouths of men; even the blues shy
At cries of children dying on deserted corners.
Jazz deserted, leaving us to our burning.

(Jazz is an African traitor.)

What one-hundred-percent redblooded savage
Wastes precious time listening to jazz
With so much important killing to do?

Silence the drums, that we may hear the burning
Of Japanese in atomic colorcinemascope,
And remember the stereophonic screaming.

MY PRECHANTEUR

In the night he comes, my prechanteur,
Singing the silent songs, enchanting songs
Of purple forest, orange woods
Where yellow flower loves yellow flower,
Green limbs budding, twice yellow
Of ebony maidens with happy eyes
In orange garments, noses that twitch
Singing songs of secret love
In dark sunless places
Illuminated only by the light
Of looks in lovers' eyes,
Witnessed only by silent animals . . .
I awake, yearning, grasping.
He is gone, my prechanteur.

PERHAPS

Should I sing a requiem, as the trap closes?
Perhaps it is more fitting to shout nonsense.

Should I run to the streets, screaming lovesongs?
Perhaps it is more consistent to honk obscenities.

Should I chew my fingernails down to my wrist?
Perhaps it is better to blow eternal jazz.

Maybe I will fold the wind into neat squares.

RESPONSE

for Eileen

Sleep, little one, sleep for me,
Sleep the deep sleep of love.
You are loved, awake or dreaming,
You are loved.

Dancing winds will sing for you,
Ancient gods will pray for you,
A poor lost poet will love you,
As stars appear
In the dark
Skies.

WHO HAS SEEN THE V

A Spanish sculptor named C
Has seen the wind.
He says it is shaped like a co
And spirals into itself and ou
That it is very heavy
And can break your toe if it
Be careful when you are mo'
It can put you in the hospital

FORGET TO NOT

Remember, poet, while gallivanting across the sky,
Skylarking, shouting, calling names . . . Walk softly.

Your footprint on rain clouds is visible to naked eyes,
Lamps barnacled to your feet refract the mirrored air.

Exotic scents of your hidden vision fly in the face of time.

Remember not to forget the dying colors of yesterday
As you inhale tomorrow's hot dream, blown from frozen lips.

Remember, you naked agent of every nothing.

I am sitting in a cell with a view of evil parallels,
Waiting thunder to splinter me into a thousand me's.
It is not enough to be in one cage with one self;
I want to sit opposite every prisoner in every hole.
Doors roll and bang, every slam a finality, bang!
The junkie disappeared into a red noise, stoning out his hell.
The odored wino congratulates himself on not smoking,
Fingerprints left lying on black inky gravestones,
Noises of pain seeping through steel walls crashing
Reach my own hurt. I become part of someone forever.
Wild accents of criminals are sweeter to me than hum of cops,
Busy battening down hatches of human souls; cargo
Destined for ports of accusations, harbors of guilt.
What do policemen eat, Socrates, still prisoner, old one?

2

Painter, paint me a crazy jail, mad water-color cells.
Poet, how old is suffering? Write it in yellow lead.
God, make me a sky on my glass ceiling. I need stars now,
To lead through this atmosphere of shrieks and private hells,
Entrances and exits, in . . . out . . . up . . . down, the civic
    seesaw.
Here – me – now – hear – me – now – always here somehow.

3

In a universe of cells—who is not in jail? Jailers.
In a world of hospitals—who is not sick? Doctors.
A golden sardine is swimming in my head.
Oh we know some things, man, about some things
Like jazz and jails and God.
Saturday is a good day to go to jail.

4

Now they give a new form, quivering jelly-like,
That proves any boy can be president of Muscatel.
They are mad at him because he's one of Them.
Gray-speckled unplanned nakedness; stinking
Fingers grasping toilet bowl. Mr. America wants to bathe.
Look! On the floor, lying across America's face—
A real movie star featured in a million newsreels.
What am I doing—feeling compassion?
When he comes out of it, he will help kill me.
He probably hates living.

5

Nuts, skin bolts, clanking in his stomach, scrambled.
His society's gone to pieces in his belly, bloated.
See the great American windmill, tilting at itself,
Good solid stock, the kind that made America drunk.
Success written all over his street-streaked ass.
Successful-type success, forty home runs in one inning.
Stop suffering, Jack, you can't fool us. We know.
This is the greatest country in the world, ain't it?
He didn't make it. Wino in Cell 3.

6

There have been too many years in this short span of mine.
My soul demands a cave of its own, like the Jain god;
Yet I must make it go on, hard like jazz, glowing
In this dark plastic jungle, land of long night, chilled.
My navel is a button to push when I want inside out.
Am I not more than a mass of entrails and rough tissue?
Must I break my bones? Drink my wine-diluted blood?
Should I dredge old sadness from my chest?
Not again,
All those ancient balls of fire, hotly swallowed, let them lie.
Let me spit breath mists of introspection, bits of me,
So that when I am gone, I shall be in the air.

7

Someone whom I am is no one.
Something I have done is nothing.
Someplace I have been is nowhere.
I am not me.
What of the answers
I must find questions for?
All these strange streets
I must find cities for,
Thank God for beatniks.

8

All night the stink of rotting people,
Fumes rising from pyres of live men,
Fill my nose with gassy disgust,
Drown my exposed eyes in tears.

9

Traveling God salesmen, bursting my ear drum
With the dullest part of a good sexy book,
Impatient for Monday and adding machines.

10

Yellow-eyed dogs whistling in evening.

11

The baby came to jail today.

12

One more day to hell, filled with floating glands.

13

The jail, a huge hollow metal cube
Hanging from the moon by a silver chain.
Someday Johnny Appleseed is going to chop it down.

14

Three long strings of light
Braided into a ray.

15

I am apprehensive about my future;
My past has turned its back on me.

16

Shadows I see, forming on the wall,
Pictures of desires protected from my own eyes.

17

After spending all night constructing a dream,
Morning came and blinded me with light.
Now I seek among mountains of crushed eggshells
For the God damned dream I never wanted.

18

Sitting here writing things on paper,
Instead of sticking the pencil into the air.

19

The Battle of Monumental Failures raging,
Both hoping for a good clean loss.

20

Now I see the night, silently overwhelming day.

21

Caught in imaginary webs of conscience,
I weep over my acts, yet believe.

22

Cities should be built on one side of the street.

23

People who can't cast shadows
Never die of freckles.

24

The end always comes last.

25

We sat at a corner table,
Devouring each other word by word,
Until nothing was left, repulsive skeletons.

26

I sit here writing, not daring to stop,
For fear of seeing what's outside my head.

27

There, Jesus, didn't hurt a bit, did it?

28

I am afraid to follow my flesh over those narrow
Wide hard soft female beds, but I do.

29

Link by link, we forged the chain.
Then, discovering the end around our necks,
We bugged out.

30

I have never seen a wild poetic loaf of bread,
But if I did, I would eat it, crust and all.

31

From how many years away does a baby come?

32

Universality, duality, totality. . . .one.

33

The defective on the floor, mumbling,
Was once a man who shouted across tables.

34

Come, help flatten a raindrop.

*Written in San Francisco City Prison
Cell 3, 1959*

61

IMAGE OF WIND

At first extra shadows seemed optical illusions,
Often used to play strange mathematical games.
Self-repeating shadows can be disconcerting to one
Accustomed to creating only one; real madness came
That day shadows began to cast people everywhere.

Only the facelessness of those people, shadow formed,
Made possible the identification most people needed
To prove to themselves that they were themselves, or
At least place themselves among those who counted,
Those who were more than just some shadow's ego, printed.

The fish played games with bows of ships,
As fishermen wove themselves into nets.

Frustrated winds bounced off brick-faced towers,
Whistling over jazzy sobbing in desperate night clubs.

Sometimes, when the wind is blowing in my hair,
I cry, because its coolness is too beautiful.

But usually, I know that rain falls anyway,
Leaving only mud puddles
To catch dead leaves as they fall.
Leaves always fall.
There is nothing to say:
The wind is in charge of lives
Tonight.

SECOND APRIL

SECOND APRIL

"Be ye not conformed to this world: but be ye transformed by the renewing of your mind." Romans 12

O man in inner basement core of me, maroon obliteration smelling futures of green anticipated comings, pasts denied, now time to thwart time, time to frieze illusionary motion on far imagined walls, stopped bleeding moondial clocks, booming out dead hours—gone . . . gone . . . gone . . . gone . . . on to second April, ash-smeared crowns, perfect, conically balanced, pyramid-peaked heads, shuddering, beamed on lead-held cylinders—on granite-flowered windows, on frigid triumphs, unmolded of shapes, assumed aspects, transparent lizards, shattered glaciers, infant mountains, formed once, all time given to disappearance, speculation, investigation of holes, rocks, caught freaks, in skin sandals, ten million light years dripped screaming, hot dust rotted eyes, ages in clawing eyes, insanities packed in century-long nights, pointed timeward to now. Hollow out trees, release captive satans, explode roses, sentence grass to death, stab rivers, rage down insane clouds, unchain snowy lamaistic peaks, dehydrate oceans, suck up deserts, nail sky to scattered earth, in air, we come, to second April.

O man, thee is onion-constructed in hot gabardine, is earth onion, too, cat, O poet, they watch, man, they eye a thing, from conception, Neal knew and it cost questioners' lives. The holy man is pimpy to our whore, out of America by God, stunned stallion, he, with Einstein on carbuncled feet, is it stopped, illusionary motion, do we go on, they watch last night's angels aborted, the sky shot up, death packed up her old kit bag, they watch, man, everything is even now, the president has translucent worms in his brain, Sappho, rolling drunks in coffee galleries, cock robin is posthumously guilty, chicken little was right all along, Vachel's basic savages drive Buicks now, God is a parking meter . . .

Session zero in, is diluted, they watch, diluted that's a thing, we have not now or ever been a member of diluted, the spoon is a cop, the door is closed, I hope Rimbaud bleeds all over my stolen pants, pants, that's a thing, they watch . . . two on four, the ration, now and . . . ever, Dylan had quadruple nuns, white stainless steel walls, moving out like an ordinary Puerto Rican, full of love and death, trapped in modern icons, forgetting to rage, as his day died, prosaic night fell, like it always does, they watch, we hide, sneak, make mad in corners, corners, that's a thing, a thing world watches things, world, that's a thing, my negro suit has jew stripes, my yarmaka was lost in a flash flood while i mattered with navajos about peyote.

Session double zero is bare floors, cannery row darkness. San Juan bare whores in young-boy brilliance, discovering balls in sources of pee . . . fried stink was lunch under the bed as the thick-wristed sailor projected Anglo-ness on Maria's wrinkled heaven, I read Sade . . . against the under of the mattress, a thing, that's a thing, they watch, tonight death is blonde, we are bending ice cubes, cubes, that's a thing, cubes, Mondrian dug, they killed him in California, injected natural wood settings and cal tech . . . Modigliani spurting . . . Naked Marys, fucking me out of my mind in triple quarter tones, on my wall sideways . . . a thing they watch, they know we break out, my bending night is ending, one second is value enough, I am forever busted.

Session last zero before one . . . is tin foil, super modern fiddlesticks, they watch, looking for things, I got mine at a one cent sale, I was Mickey Finned with striped tooth paste, caught freak in twisted skin and sandals, covered with angry dust, entrails of lorn . . . women hanging in my alien lips, let me embarrass me, expose self in my self, too cool for the soft blow, hard, not hard enough, they watch, dense bartenders with godhead in legal bodies, they watch, not seeing us in bubblegum wrappers, in hands of future monsters, future, that's a thing, future men with three penises seducing future women with vaginas in their armpits, future children with lavender eyes between their toes, wiping crazy fallout from the ass on their future skulls, a thing, future.

Session golden horn before one . . . is Bayou St. John, Big Sur pornography dipped in, emptied . . . a thing, dipped, dipped in poems, the black child glistened in self-conceived madness . . . dipped in contemporary multiplied generations, played musical electric chairs, dipped in in-jazz the Kansas City maniac found world three, Zulu laughter, good old Fourth of July American heroin, Sumeria, Picasso modern limericks, madness, final mausoleums . . . ah . . . leu . . . cha . . . the time is now . . . is a thing, time is . . . they watch . . .

Session zero before green . . . is head of cows in Montana, Indians pushing history on freeways, look out for green, they watch, hidden matchbook covers, secret chronicles of our time . . . a thing, time, pasted on roof of mouth, time uses needles, hooked time, booming out orgasmic time, plastered on cottony mattresses, they watch, small private pelvic mushrooms.

Session semi-zero before inverted fraction . . . is a five thing and strategic incisions, one-o, two-o, three-o, four-o, five-o snips for veal cutlets, paper signing papas . . . a thing, O god, let me use your library card, I want the OxforD BooK oF ModerN JazZ . . . I want Baudelaire's Denunciation of Moses, I want Ezra Pound's Life of George Washington, I want Stark-weather's Biography of Billy Graham, let me steal James Dean's suicide note from the film division, I need the Intelligent Woman's Guide to Mongrelism, I need Greenwich Village Novels to wipe me with, I need New York Times Index to count the murders, I need to talk with fly pages, that's a thing now, fly pages . . . o fly, o so higho fly, they watch, put spaghetti in the octane, the new bomb is clean, thank God for soaP.

Session quarter zero . . . is tubercular leaves, chipped nose saints, alabaster sphinx cats . . . burning warehouses, nonchalant cops, pop-bopping black leather angels, fathered fathers, good daddy doctors . . . a thing, daddies . . . they watch, belly paroles, bareskin eagles . . . numbers of highway dark things . . . impersonal billboard watches, strips, cut quilting blocks, torn gloves, long thin drinks of water in bulging supporters, supporters . . . a thing . . . support march of dollar and a halfs, support sisterhood of Christian and Bantus, it's a thing, they watch for things, we sand things, before glassthings . . . soon ash things, later everything, stupid gums bleed needlessly on hard skin apples, is the old god lying in the cave, pumping stations never close.

Session eight before nothing . . . is bales of cardinal hats, oversexed rabbis, used car sex, Boston dreams of cobwebs, sobwebs, Himalayan streetcar tracks, did the mother die of jazz . . . they . . . watch . . . of is thing, it's all of, pockets full of light years on strange borders, recording enterings and leaving, hung things, zentree mess of whoring through tree branches . . . unforgotten bites, mouths full of longhair, wait, don't break the corduroy, but look out for green, glue the limb first, she too old to lay on cold, use ladders, take bottle caps, bathing caps and caps of Caribbe waves and when the Fall came, everybody fucked his girl.

Session nothing before nothing . . . is red, look out for green, Dante's blanket too, a thing, lilies burn crisply on green screaming mornings, dogs licking backs of necks, fountains full of sacramental wind and Yom Kippur Good Friday drinking in wet shoes, electric spitballs of lying, Roman night of baby boy dreams, musclebound streets, all our eye, things cork-screwing raindrop pressures, sacrificed goats, queer witch doctors, inventions, frosty gray pocket of peace, linen courtyard of up and down skin piling into cores of new earths, bitch bites and fingernail communiques, God calling and ceiling guffaws, pushed back clots of unformed nothing, needle me dragged into illusion, God make me a tree.

Session nothing . . . is drunken funerals, pubic breakfasts, football player sex in Saturday milk bottles, flight and attempt to raid marble quarry, stone and, on with gold fillings, lost forever in shriveled nipple hysterically conceived combination of fingershaped genitals, auto-sculpted explosions of images of explosions exploded.

Session one . . . is hospitalgram, in-group shrieks, narcocomalts, ripped lung leaking coughed air, banana peels, sad significances, unknown fuckers, curly teeth, tea-angry gums holding defeated teeth, fingers holding hands, feet-shaped organs, turning against, inside. Terror-love, falling ceilings, and me you falling too, between legs, arms, members, we are each other's members.

Session two . . . is finally escaped dreams, they watch now, day over night into day—only nuns at night, and light itself is satire time, Tuesday wants out, chickened night, for day, one day this week, no, Jack Karowack, don't break into Mill Valley jails with your shoes on, walls rain all time, but, comic it, baby—love—cool new Indian corn every winter is our lot, and lockos, damn, wham, bamm, cool.

Session three . . . is crazy machine broken, darts not arrived yet, so love, no empty thick concave bottles sing tonight, shadows come too, in new faces, gassed cracked glasses crack, no break, wiser grown kneecaps, third eye remains basic, two birds cheated, punishment until new bathroom arrives, grass will stay, Africa-faced and new mud on the bed-o.

Session four . . . is poor busted Santa Claus, back to hot toys again. They watch, very red, look out for green, eating going on despite no food, facial limp coming back, independent lips, new thing, they watch, ones with babes, boring in judging Colas—screams are rattles to dogs, tears real popular, broken legs have new meaning too—cane on floor, cracking under footprint, horn slurring. Commemorate, question eyewitness pavement, coming is an event, stinging continues.

Session five . . . is in getting out, four times is five, we hope not . . . psychodramatics of long thin stuff calling caterwauling, hoarse whistles in deepness of breathy ears, tonguing old children, flood survivors, deep in jungles, elevating up in flood reactions and objectively conceived esteem, caution, too, is new thing, they watch, ones with babes, boring in juding is tomorrow, thin circles over eyes, trust no longer trusts us, paper is now thick and assy like brown, wrong is good is sad is glad is mad.

Session six . . . is cancered doctors, rejected volunteers, too young, two lungs, too far away for searching, eyes ransacked first, naturalized afterbirths, no problems, fear blows too, strips of mother hate, we get in tonight, problem out now, silver is not spoons only, dress event now, god getting married, funny fun in cassocks, and hoods too, spitballs spiked on ribs are attractive abstracts eating poets, they watch, God eats crying, smooth nine month grave faces, bent, me, you, man, thirsting.

Session seven . . . they watch, we shout, they catch, pushing, bluing, swinging, digging, He won't say, they wash windows, we break them and windows breaking us, fresh lobes to come drunker, they watch, look out for green, we drink drunker fumes, look out for green, smoke god damn soppy wet on the floor toilet paper.

70

Session eight ... is Hindu baby in tiger suit, they don't know, see draggy khaki, folded three inside canvas, three pounds of color, three toes flattened, that's a thing now, numbers ... five cheats, three's goo-o, eight cannot be trusted, ten's the queer count, colors, all. They see ... numbers, we party, leader died, we commemorate, new on old they see us, multiplication, that's a thing, we be three free, see, be, they see our stained noses, we count up doubled-up hairs, folding near middle, they confer, locking us in our noses, we smuggle, giggle ... struggle, they guard, they guard God, throwing strips of fore- skin, that's a thing, t.b., t.v., t.d., v.d., p.d. .... cowboy boots, big busses, signs oleomarginality, stereoriginality ... hi-finali- ties, they can't fall us, already we in blank a book, crank a crook, indeed do a deed, turning a key, door faced, mousing in, we stay, they manage, we brain out.

Session nine ... they watch outside suicide, death you is our woman now, look out for green ... that's a thing, they watch things, reports we can't smash wheat, they make bread, stale crusty bitey bread, we cause, they catch, the bridge, they don't see it, hidden in magazines ... concealed in blendozines, bleedozines, killograms, echopium, good, good fish, crocker- faced ... look out for green, catch a color, look out for num- bers, they bite numbers, we bite them ... they question us, we answer them, spit, black, blue, inside a spiral, a whirl, cross around ... only one conversation, the world ends, the unworld begins, they watch, we urinate, going ... now the tiptoe we hear, we all rolling, they unfill the pie, fling oatmeal to the air, breakfast is a new thing, he's new, bleeding hand, prints on a white wall, that's a thing.

Session ten ... burning burns on burned hand, that's a thing a thing, down to ten thousand wounds ... they watch, we swap watches, we chew time, they chew us, chewing, that's a thing, a new thing, chewing, everybody chew somebody, everybody chew a dog, cats exempt, numbers too ... they watch, a dusty window, hell my eyes, bell my tongue, we are attacking our hair, it waves to neighbors in skies, kinky relatives, wrapped in comets, a thing, comets . . . aluminum cheats, deflects, cities deflected, they watch, we cross breed eyelids, gas helps, it gets us, they get us, we get no getting, we erase ourselves, we smear our board, we are gone, they watch, we cook old chaplinesque shoestrings, they watch, we have never, have we, never ever, never.

Session eleven . . . they conceal our eyeteeth in garter belts, we assume presumptions, report proportions, we tear at his wounds, see, the boy bleeds, but look out for green, they watch, we steal a desert, drown a car, kidnap a mountain, anti-social a girl, they watch, we tar roofs to sit under sun on, a thing, suns, the sun is hot blooded, we o, so cold, cold blood monkeys never kill, not even for food, they bred it out, they bread it out, they bread it . . . new catchy tune, love a chunk of bread, love a hunk of bread, love a funk of dead, head . . . o, me, we, they, trapped in a polka dot . . . caught in porcelain pot, clomping on the floor of ice, that's a thing, floors, ground falling out, indoors, we know they watch, look out for green, they pan out, we go to the great rain forest.

Session twelve . . . a mom pop, on the part they don't see, poor pores sucking in bad air . . . a thing, air, the air, distended air, hard air, air of twin birds on looney peaks . . . air too is a thing, not a goose, they watch, funky circuses parading elephants across airy clouds of air, they watch, we take chances, we give chances . . . they watch, we are raffled off, out, a thing, out, close out, far out, in, out and out, and new is out, too, the first father, on the ship, out in air, cheating at cards of air, all we are is, all we are is, air we are in a hole in space, we put it in, they watch . . . we take it out, the taste of dust on breast is odored air on pricking tongues sticking air and mounds of hair stuck on light, grainless blocks of wood, staggering down the night, they watch the air, we disappear, into a quick dab for clean, splintering, too, now.

Session thirteen . . . is a metal thing, foot-stomach thing, bent prong fork, turning up, on, in, they watch metal, pictures of metal, up through lower holes through stratospheric sex, and metallic jazz, but look out for green, a thing, look, they watch, look, look into the face of a road, see brightly striped freaks paved into dividing lines, a thing, lines, they watch lines, long lines of watchers watching lines, they dig straight, they . . . unbended lines sinking to bottom of earth, we printing many suicide notes on moon-shaped traffic lights, they panel room-shaped metal caves with old skin trophies, we wave dramatic underwear from bent flag poles, they watch, build things, inside trees, clean restrooms in pregnant redwood bellies.

Session fourteen . . . is a roach and happy guts, shorn hair of minor criminals, on floors of prefabricated gas chambers, we mad on Aztec planted turnips, read poems off each other's ass by narrow daylight in New Tex hotel rooms, they watch, we unzip fly, why, gasping into our own interiors, hoping to drag air to strange tomb-like bellies . . . they watch tombs, we throw soggy peanut shells under skidding wheels, we witness God's divorce, the bitch leaves, we cry jazz historical tears, they watch, we lock door on bankrupt, God give us new, we ate fire last time, be cool, God.

Session fifteen . . . is explosive drops of water, on masks, on faces, on, nothing, sounds of life strangled in our stomachs, whimpering in our heads, dramatic little realities, through stained glass, rouged Virgin Marys signal a left turn on, a thing on is, they watch On, we overwhelm with mad babies raving down slippery parallelic bars, we go to On museum to see ancient Ons, screaming into Ludwig's cupped ear for a well built death mask, or a four bar get high, or a promise of remembrance in sexy cures, they, watch, on corners, in opinionated, finny, gaudy wombs, power driven, they watch, we wrap each fume in separate paper for the trip we are constantly making, Oh, the god bus has a busted wheel, wheel's a thing they watch, whirling wheels, wailing wheels, steel wheels, cardboard wheels, real wheels, they watch, we crazy and go glowing in pointed spinning soft flames, disappearing into heads of candles, they watch.

We watch them going on watching us going on going, wrapped in pink barley leaves, almost, the time is not near, but, nearer we are to time, and time nearer to ticks. Burning in torch surrender to auto-fantasy, we illuminate the hidden December, seen, flamelit in the on core of the second April, come for the skeleton of time.

> Kissed at wintertide, alone in a lemming world,
> Green bitches, harlequin men, shadowed babes,
> Dumped on the galvez greens, burned with grass.

ABOMUNIST MANIFESTO
by Bomkauf

ABOMUNIST MANIFESTO

ABOMUNISTS JOIN NOTHING BUT THEIR HANDS OR LEGS,
OR OTHER SAME.

ABOMUNISTS SPIT ANTI-POETRY FOR POETIC REASONS
AND FRINK.

ABOMUNISTS DO NOT LOOK AT PICTURES PAINTED
BY PRESIDENTS AND UNEMPLOYED PRIME MINISTERS.

IN TIMES OF NATIONAL PERIL, ABOMUNISTS, AS REALITY
AMERICANS, STAND READY TO DRINK THEMSELVES
TO DEATH FOR THEIR COUNTRY.

ABOMUNISTS DO NOT FEEL PAIN, NO MATTER HOW MUCH
IT HURTS.

ABOMUNISTS DO NOT USE THE WORD SQUARE EXCEPT WHEN
TALKING TO SQUARES.

ABOMUNISTS READ NEWSPAPERS ONLY TO ASCERTAIN THEIR
ABOMINUBILITY.

ABOMUNISTS NEVER CARRY MORE THAN FIFTY DOLLARS
IN DEBTS ON THEM.

ABOMUNISTS BELIEVE THAT THE SOLUTION OF PROBLEMS
OF RELIGIOUS BIGOTRY IS, TO HAVE A CATHOLIC
CANDIDATE FOR PRESIDENT AND A PROTESTANT
CANDIDATE FOR POPE.

ABOMUNISTS DO NOT WRITE FOR MONEY; THEY WRITE
THE MONEY ITSELF.

ABOMUNISTS BELIEVE ONLY WHAT THEY DREAM ONLY
AFTER IT COMES TRUE.

ABOMUNIST CHILDREN MUST BE REARED ABOMUNIBLY.

ABOMUNIST POETS, CONFIDENT THAT THE NEW LITERARY
FORM "FOOT-PRINTISM" HAS FREED THE ARTIST
OF OUTMODED RESTRICTIONS, SUCH AS: THE ABILITY TO

READ AND WRITE, OR THE DESIRE TO COMMUNICATE,
MUST BE PREPARED TO READ THEIR WORK AT DENTAL
COLLEGES, EMBALMING SCHOOLS, HOMES FOR UNWED
MOTHERS, HOMES FOR WED MOTHERS, INSANE ASYLUMS,
USO CANTEENS, KINDERGARTENS, AND COUNTY JAILS.
ABOMUNISTS NEVER COMPROMISE THEIR REJECTIONARY
PHILOSOPHY.

ABOMUNISTS REJECT EVERYTHING EXCEPT SNOWMEN.

NOTES DIS- AND RE- GARDING ABOMUNISM

Abomunism was founded by Barabbas, inspired by his dying
    words: "I wanted to be in the middle, but I went too
    far out."
Abomunism's main function is to unite the soul with oatmeal
    cookies.
Abomunists love love, hate hate, drink drinks, smoke smokes,
    live lives, die deaths.
Abomunist writers write writing, or nothing at all.
Abomunist poetry, in order to be compleatly (Eng. sp.)
    understood, should be eaten . . . except on fast days,
    slow days, and mornings of executions.
Abomunists, could they be a color, would be green,
    and tell everyone to go.
Uncrazy Abomunists crazy unAbomunists by proxy kicky
    tricks, as follows:
    By telling psychometric poets two heads are better
      than none.
    By selling middle names to impotent personnel
      managers.
    By giving children brightly wrapped candy fathers.
    By biting their own hands after feeding themselves.
    By calling taxis dirty names, while ordering fifths
      of milk.
    By walking across hills, ignoring up and down.
    By giving telescopes to peeping Toms.
    By using real names at false hotels.

Abomunists who feel their faith weakening will have to
    spend two weeks in Los Angeles.
When attacked, Abomunists think positive, repeating over
    and under: "If I were a crime, I'd want to be
    committed . . .
            No! . . . Wait!"

FURTHER NOTES

(*taken from* "Abomunismus und Religion" *by Tom Man*)

Krishnamurti can relax the muscles of your soul,
Free your aching jawbone from the chewinggum habit.
Ouspensky can churn your illusions into butter and
Give you circles to carry them in, around your head.
Subud can lock you in strange rooms with vocal balms
And make your ignorant clothing understand you.
Zen can cause changes in the texture of your hair,
Removing you from the clutches of sexy barbers.
Edgar Cayce can locate your gallstones, other organs,
On the anarchistic rockpiles of Sacramento.
Voodoo Marie can give you Loas, abstract horses,
Snorting guides to tar-baby black masses.
Billy can plug you into the Christ machine. Mail in your
Mind today. Hurry, bargain God week, lasts one week only.

$$ ABOMUNUS CRAXIOMS $$

Egyptian mummies are lousy dancers.
        Alcoholics cannot make it on root beer.
Jazz never made it back down the river.
        Licking postage stamps depletes the body fluids.
Fat automobiles laugh more than others, and frink.
        Men who die in wars become seagulls and fly.
Roaches have a rough time of it from birth.
        People who read are not happy.

People who do not read are not happy.
People are not very happy.
These days people get sicker quicker.
The sky is less crowded in the West.
Psychiatrists pretend not to know everything.
Way out people know the way out.
Laughter sounds orange at night, because
reality is unrealizable while it exists.
Abomunists knew it all along,
but couldn't get the butterscotch down.

EXCERPTS FROM THE LEXICON ABOMUNON

At election time, Abomunists frink more, and naturally, as hard-core Abo's, we feel the need to express ourselves somewhat more abomunably than others. We do this simply by not expressing ourselves (abomunization). We do not express ourselves in the following terms:

Abommunity: n. Grant Avenue & other frinky places.

Abomunarcosis: n. Addiction to oatmeal cookies & liverwurst.

Abomunasium: n. Place in which abomunastics occur, such as bars, coffee shops, USO's, juvenile homes, pads, etc.

Abomunastics: n. Physical Abomunism.

Abomunate, The: n. The apolitical CORPUS ABOMUNISMUS.

Abomunette: n. Female type Abomunist (rare).

Abomunibble: v. 1. To bite a daisy. 2. How poets eat.

Abomunicate: v. To dig. (Slang: to frink.)

Abomunics: n. Abomunistic techniques.

Abomunificance: n. The façade behind the reality of double-talking billboards.

Abomunify: v. To (censored) with an Abomunette, or vice versa.

Abomunik: n. Square abomuflack.

Abomunism: n. Footprintism. A rejectory philosophy founded by Barabbas and dedicated to the proposition that the essence of existence is reality essential and neither four-sided nor frinky, but not non-frinky either.

Abomunist: n. One who avows Abomunism, disavowing almost everything else, especially butterscotch.

Abomunitions: n. Love, commonly found in the plural state, very.

Abomunity: n. A by-product of abomunarcosis, also obtained by frinking. (Thus: Frinkism.)

Abomunize: v. To carefully disorganize—usually associated with frinking.

Abomunoid: adj. Having some Abomunistic qualities such as tragictories, pail faces, or night vision.

Abomunology: n. The systematic study of Abomunism; classes every other Frinksday, 2 a.m.

Abomunosis: n. Sweet breath.

Abomunosophy: n. Theoretical Abomunism.

Abomunull: n. 1. They. 2. One who is not quite *here.*

Abomusical: adj. Diggable sounds.

Abomutiny: n. Regimentation. v. To impose organization from without, i.e., without oatmeal cookies.

Frink: v. To (censored). n. (censored) and (censored).

Frinkism: n. A sub-cult of Abomunism, not authorized nor given abomunitude by Bomkauf.

Frinky: adj. Like (censored).

—Compiled by BIMGO

ABOMUNIST ELECTION MANIFESTO

1. Abomunists vote against everyone by not voting for anyone.
2. The only proposition Abomunists support are those made to members of the opposite sex.
3. Abomunists demand the abolition of Oakland.
4. Abomunists demand low-cost housing for homosexuals.
5. Abomunists demand suppression of illegal milk traffic.
6. Abomunists demand statehood for North Beach.
7. The only office Abomunists run for is the unemployment office.

8. Abomunists support universal frinkage.
9. Abomunists demand split-level ranch-type phonebooths.
10. Abomunists demand the reestablishment of the government in its rightful home at **?**

STILL FURTHER NOTES
DIS- & RE- GARDING ABOMUNISM

The following translation is the first publication of the Live Sea Scrolls, found by an old Arab oilwell driller. He first saw them on the dead beds of the live sea. Thinking they were ancient bubblegum wrappers he took them to town to trade in for hashish coupons. As chance would have it, the hashish pipes were in the hands of a visiting American relief official, who reluctantly surrendered them in return for two villages and a canal. We developed the cunic script by smearing it with tanfastic sun lotion, after which we took it down to the laundromat and placed it in the dryer for two hours ($1.20). We then ate four pounds of garlic bread & frinked; then we translated this diary. We feel this is one of the oldest Abomunist documents yet discovered.

MONDAY—B.C.—minus 4—10 o'sun, a.m.

Nazareth getting too hot, fuzz broke up two of my poetry readings last night. Beat vagrancy charge by carrying my toolbox to court—carpenters O.K. Splitting to Jeru. as soon as I get wheels.

TUESDAY—B.C.—minus 3—8 o'sun, p.m.

Jeru. cool, Roman fuzz busy having a ball, never bother you unless someone complains. Had a ball this morning, eighty-sixed some square bankers from the Temple, read long poem on revolt. Noticed cats taking notes, maybe they are publisher's agents, hope so, it would be crazy to publish with one of those big Roman firms.

WEDNESDAY—B.C.—minus 2—11 o'sun, a.m.

Local poets and literary people throwing a big dinner for me tonight, which should be a gas. Most of the cats here real cool, writing real far out—only cat bugs me is this Judas, got shook up when I refused to loan him thirty pieces of silver, he seems to be hung on loot, must be a lush.

THURSDAY—B.C.—minus 1—10 o'sun, p.m.

I am writing this in my cell. I was framed. How can they give the death sentence on charges of disorderly conduct and having public readings without a permit? It's beyond me. Oh well, there's always hope. Maybe that lawyer Judas is getting me can swing it. If he can't, God help me.

FRIDAY—Neutral—5 o'sun, a.m.

Roman turnkey was around passing out crosses. The two thieves have good connections so they got first crack at them —I got stuck with the biggest one. One of the guards doesn't dig my beard and sandals—taunted me all night. I'm going to be cool now, but tomorrow I'll tell him to go to hell, and what's so groovy is: he will. . . . somebody coming. I feel sort of abomunable. Barabbas gets a suspended sentence and I make the hill. What a drag. Well, that's poetry, and I've got to split now.

BOMS

1. Stashed in his minaret, towering
   Over the hashish wells, Caliph
   Ralph inventoried his popcorn hoard
   While nutty eunuchs conced his concubines.

2. Movies about inventors' lives and glass-encased
   historical documents do not move me as much as
   drinking or hiccupping in the bathtub.

3. Filled with green courage we sneezed political,
   Coughing our dirty fingernails for President.

4. Ageless brilliant colored spiders webbing eternally,
   Instead of taking showers under the fire hydrants
   in summer.

5. Unruly hairs in the noses of statues in public gardens
   Were placed there by God in a fit of insane jealousy.

6. Single-breasted suits, dancing in the air,
   Turned up their cuffs at double-breasted suits
   Plodding down the street.

7. Greedy burglars stole my mother and father,
   And gave me a free pass to the circus and I like stripes.

8. Misty-eyed, knee-quaking me, gazing on the family
   Home,
   Realizing that I was about to burn it down.

9. Waterspouts, concealed in pig knuckle barrels, rumbled,
   As tired storms whispered encouragement.

10. Angry motives scrambled for seating space,
    Shaking their fist at the moon.

11. Liver salesmen door to doored back pats,
    Disturbing chimneysweeps sleeping on roofs.

12. Daily papers suicided from tree tops,
    Purpling the lawn with blueprints.

13. Caribou pranced in suburban carports,
    Hoofmarking the auto-suggestions.

14. Pentagonal merit badges flowed
    Gracefully over the male nurses' heads.

15. Disordered aquariums, dressed in shredded wheat,
    Delivered bibles to pickles crying in confessionals.

ABOMUNIST RATIONAL ANTHEM

(to be sung before and after frinking)

Derrat slegelations, flo goof babereo
Sorash sho dubies, wago, wailo, wailo.

Geed bop nava glid, nava glied, nava
Speerieder, huyedist, hedacaz, ax, O, O.

Deeredition, Boomedition, squom, squom, squom,
Dee beetstrawist, wapago, wapago, loco,
       locoro, locoest
Voometeyereepetiop, bop, bop, bop, whipop.

Dearat, shloho, kurritip, plog, mangi, squom pot,
Clopo jago, bree, bree, asloopered, akingo labiop,
Engpop, engpop, boint plolo, plolo, bop bop.

(Music composed by Schroeder.)

ABOMUNIST DOCUMENTS

(discovered during ceremonies at the Tomb of the Unknown Draftdodger)

Boston, December 1773

Dear Adams:

I am down to my last can of tea, and cannot afford to score for more as the British Pushers have stamped a new tax on the Stuff, I know that many Colony Cats are as hung as I am, so

why don't we get together on the Night of the Sixteenth and
Go down to the Wharf and swing with a few Pounds. I think
it will be cooler if we make the Scene dressed as Indians, the
British Fuzz, will not know who the Tea-Heads are, it will be
very dark so we will have to carry torches, tell the Cats not to
goof with the torches and start a Fire, that would ruin the
whole Scene.

Later,

HANCOCK

West Point, December 1778

Dear Wife:

I am trying my best to raise the Money for the Rent, but the
Army has no funds for Personal Hardships, I sounded George
about Promotion, but the Virginia Crowd seems to be in Con
trol so even my hero status can't be any good. Met a very
nice English Cat named André, and he has offered to see if he
can swing a Loan for me, I don't know where he can get so
much money, but since he has been so nice, it would be
traitorous to ask.

P.S. He was telling me how much cheaper it is to live in Eng
land. Maybe when this is over we can settle there. I have been
doing a lot of drawing in my spare time, and tonight I prom
ised to show André some of my sketches, if I can find them
they are all mixed up with my defense plans and I've broken
my glasses. Have to close now. I can hear André sneaking in
the chances he takes. He really loves Art.

Yours, faithfully,

BENEDICT

ABOMNEWSCAST . . . ON THE HOUR . . .

America collides with iceberg piloted by Lindbergh
baby. . . .Aimee Semple Macpherson, former dictator of
California, discovered in voodoo nunnery disguised as
Moby Dick. . . .New hit song sweeping the country, the
Leopold & Loeb Cha-cha-cha. . . .Pontius Pilate loses
no-hitter on an error, league split over scorer's decision,
Hebrew fireballer out for season with injured hands. . . .
Civilian Defense Headquarters unveils new bomb shelter
with two-car garage, complete with indoor patio and
barbecue unit that operates on radioactivity, comes in
decorator colors, no down payment for vets, to be sold only
to those willing to sign loyalty oath. . . .Forest Lawn
Cemetery opens new subdivision of split-level tombs for
middle-income group. . . .President inaugurates new policy of
aggressive leadership, declares December 25th Christmas
Day. . . .Pope may allow priests to marry, said to be
aiming at one big holy family. . . .Norman Rockwell cover,
"The Lynching Bee" from "Post" Americana series, wins
D.A.R. Americanism award. . . .Russians said to be copying
TV format with frontier epic filmed in Berlin, nuclear
Wagon Train features Moiseyev Dancers. . . .Red China
cuts birthrate drastically, blessed events plummet to two
hundred million a year. . . .Cubans seize Cuba, outraged
U.S. acts quickly, cuts off tourist quota, administration
introduces measure to confine all rhumba bands to detention
camps during emergency. . . .Both sides in Cold War stock-
piling atomic missiles to preserve peace, end of mankind
seen if peace is declared, UN sees encouraging sign in
small war policy, works quietly for wider participation
among backward nations. . . .End of news. . . .Remember your
national emergency signal, when you see one small
mushroom cloud and three large ones, it is not a drill,
turn the TV off and get under it. . . . Foregoing sponsored
by your friendly neighborhood Abomunist. . . .Tune in
next world. . . .

New Directions Paperbooks – A Partial Listing

For complete listing request free catalog from
New Directions, 80 Eighth Avenue, New York 10011   † Bilingual

For complete listing request free catalog from
New Directions, 80 Eighth Avenue, New York 10011

† Bilingual